The Awakening Of Man

HAMLET

Shakespeare's Message

John Stubbs

Illustrations by
Kevin Watts

Copyright © John Stubbs 2014
All rights reserved

ISBN 978-0-9769732-8-7

*When you understand Shakespeare,
he produces a state of amazement in you.*

Robert E. Burton

CHAPTER 1
Sacred Messages in Art

People have sought the spiritual secrets of life and death throughout the ages. In very ancient times schools of awakening were openly spread over the Earth, and their initiates led open spiritual lives within their communities. The knowledge was transmitted by word of mouth and demonstration – inner meanings and psychic truths being revealed directly to each seeker according to his capacity.

In those days psychology, spirituality, and religion were one and the same thing. Nature was revered, and natural formations were seen as embodying inner spiritual truths. Mountains implied ascent to a higher, godly state, their size instilling humility and reverence, each valley representing a temporary setback followed by a return to the spiritual path. Caves signified entry into the unknown, the overcoming of fear and the quiet stillness of solitude. Rocks and cliffs symbolised rugged virtues and beacons of encouragement on the spiritual path. Trees displayed long steady growth and the rewards of patience. Above all, the silence of Nature indicated the subtle aspect of spiritual transformation.

But the age of war and conflict arrived on Earth; men grew cold and more calculating. Schools started to disappear. Rulers who had benevolently reigned over their subjects were overthrown by warriors or replaced by schemers. The new leaders saw schools as a threat to their power and authority. Initiates were lost and many others that survived did not receive sufficient training. Sacred esoteric knowledge started to disappear, or worse, became corrupted or replaced by personal inventions.

Then something extraordinary happened. In the sixth century BC military campaigns spread throughout the Middle East from Babylon and threw many men together into that small corner of the world. This went on for nearly a century. For instance, Nebuchadnezzar II swept in two waves across the region, the second in 597 BC, capturing many. It is best known as the period of captivity of the Jews, but other nations were also overrun. In Egypt, for example, Pythagoras the Greek, an advanced spiritual man, was taken in 525 BC by Cambyses II (King of Babylon by that time).

At a point which may be unique in human history, many spiritual men from many nations were thrown together in one place. Ancient methods of passing esoteric knowledge no longer worked, and they could see that it was gradually being lost. Through discussion and experiment they developed stratagems to preserve the knowledge and transmit it unnoticeably to future generations.

They realised that it had to be inserted in forms which were impervious to manipulations. Ideally, its preservation would be assured for as long as the encompassing forms survived, even if those forms were distorted or partially destroyed. And most importantly, the forms had to have a long-lasting endurance.

Open plain language could not be used. Plain language is in any case a poor means to convey subtle inner truths. Words are understood differently by different people, even if only slightly, and they change their meanings over time. Each concept has to be clearly defined in terms of other, unclear words. Instead of the direct experience of spiritual states one has descriptions of states, which is not at all the same thing. Descriptions can be easily 'corrected' to suit the ends of the authorities, and finally, translation into other languages depends upon the subjective nature of the translators.

The Bible is a example of subjective translation. But its inner meaning escaped these manipulations, as we shall see.

In essence, the means of communicating esoteric truth had to bypass the ordinary way people took in information both then and today – ordinary language merely evoking the perceptual processes that see the external world through conventional lenses. An inner esoteric truth must touch the spiritual centre of a person, even though in the beginning he might not be personally aware of it.

So these regenerate men of Babylon selected already existing forms that could be used to secrete inner messages, and then they determined how the messages could be hidden.

So what were these forms?

In place of the mountains revered in more ancient times, *architecture* could convey messages, both in its overall form, and in the shapes and details of its structures. Instead of rocks, *sculptures* could be used with subtly modified details that did not detract from the overall purpose. Cliffs and caves could be replaced by *temples*, and so on.

Painted pictures and images, which already had a visual allurement of their own, could incorporate subtle signs and symbols without affecting their overall impact.

Dances and Rituals could include encoded aspects of the inner knowledge while maintaining their outer form.

And finally, texts themselves could also carry the knowledge, but packaged in stories. Passing beyond mere language, stories could describe heroic events, whether legendary, fantastic or mythological, and messages could be embedded in them in ways not immediately apparent.

With regard to long endurance, architectures and sculptures used stone or geographic locations of spiritual significance. The pyramids and other great structures in Egypt are obvious examples using stone. The mountains of Tibet or of Machu Picchu in Peru are examples using geographic locations where temples and other structures have been built, partly to direct your attention to those mountains.

Paintings, images, dances and rituals were used in an overall context which itself is so important or loved by people that they naturally maintained them in that context. People already had folklore within which they maintained many traditions and sacred objects. But folklore is dependent on ethnic groups and something wider was needed.

This wider context was *religion*, and indeed this is where the texts became doubly or even multiply useful, because not only did they serve as religious instruction and guidance, but they were also carriers of hidden esoteric messages.

Like folklore, religious paintings and texts representing beliefs and practices beyond individual human lives, were zealously preserved by people in their original form without the inner messages necessarily being understood. They were even instructed to preserve the form by words in the texts. In the same vein dances portraying such stories could contain messages.

Religious rituals such as baptism, the coming of age, betrothal, wedding and funeral also provided vehicles.

Mountain seen through temple window - Machu Picchu – Peru

And so it was. It is said that the first five books of the Bible, the Torah, were set down in written form at this time of history, although many stories within them were already very well-known. In a sense, these writings also defined the authority of religion from then on, and for this reason they became precious to self-assigned priests. Human mentality was growing more attached to concrete forms as part of its general descent into materiality.

These and other scriptures in the Bible are examples of texts containing objective messages behind the stories in addition to their more obvious historical, religious and moral content.

And so it continued until today. Over the centuries, countless artists and artisans have produced works that contained esoteric messages. Works which come to mind are paintings by Leonardo da Vinci, Rembrandt or Botticelli, and the great works of architecture such as the Taj Mahal and the Gothic cathedrals. Esoteric stories were written to fascinate as well as educate, such as those written by Hans Andersen. Fairy stories and epic poems holding esoteric meanings are perhaps the oldest forms ever used and were transmitted by word of mouth for millennia. The epic of Gilgamesh is an example.

The authors introduced subtle anomalies into their creations, which would usually be passed over or dismissed as little mistakes or whims of the artist, or explainable by the supernatural nature of the subject (such as Christ walking on water in the text of the New Testament).

These anomalies were the triggers. They alerted the attentive observer to the existence of an inner message; and their many repetitions in different guises in the work assured the observer that he had indeed 'opened the box'.

There are also many levels of meaning in sacred texts. All the levels are valid, each level being appropriate for people of different natures and capacities, and all meanings can exist simultaneously. Dante described four main levels of meaning, namely: Literal; Allegorical (metaphorical); Moral (religious); and Anagogical (the inner esoteric message). But there are also shades within these.

CHAPTER 2
The Art of Shakespeare

Shakespeare was almost certainly aware of this when he wrote his plays (a total of thirty seven are attributed to him). Certainly his later plays and his sonnets were written with more urgency and intensity. These works do not just entertain and fascinate, they carry inner messages about awakening the true spirit of man — and even how to awaken it.

In the extraordinary book, "The Secret of Shakespeare", Martin Lings approaches Shakespeare's plays as works of sacred art and describes *Hamlet* as being Shakespeare's first play purely devoted to the message of unfolding spiritual awareness. We shall go deeper into *Hamlet* soon, but let us touch on Shakespeare's works in general for the moment.

Generally, what they are implying can be lumped into one basic message: *You are not who you think you are.* You have forgotten who you are and you are just happy to be an ordinary day-to-day person, doing your job, earning a living, having successes and failures and living your life.

Or maybe you are not so happy but so what? Who

can expect to be happy all the time? Isn't that what life is all about? Enjoying what you can and bearing the rest.

No, Shakespeare says, there is something extra. There is the prize you have forgotten to pick up: your birthright, your inheritance, what was with you since the day you were born — the "pearl of great price". He mentions this in his literature in many different ways. For example, in sonnet 74 he says:

> *The worth of that, is that which it contains,*
> *And that is this, and this with thee remains.*

In other words what you have within you is much more valuable than your everyday self. And furthermore, the second line tells you *how to recognise it* if you read it properly. Commonly we would think that the words "And that is this" refer to the sonnet itself. And they do, but it also has another meaning, because in the split-second you realise that it is You who is looking at the word *"this"* so it means the real you is present! But it all goes in a flash – your customary thought processes take over and you have a thought about it – and thoughts destroy that very delicate state. So – do not think, do not wonder – just stop, and know.

But don't worry, you did not lose it – *it with thee remains*. The next time you realise such a profound truth you will get it again. But holding that fleeting state is very difficult, and if you do not constantly practise to control your mental tendencies or you continually indulge your everyday self, you will not be able to keep it. In sonnet 16 Shakespeare says:

> *But wherefore do not you a mightier way,*
> *Make war upon this bloody tyrant Time?*

"This bloody tyrant Time" is your daily, petty life, your everyday self, which I shall call the *lower self*[1*] from now on.

So now, supposing that you accept that maybe he has a point, and supposing that you do wish to discover who you really are and want to go through your life as your real self, what can you do? The play *Hamlet* doesn't seem to say much about that on the face of it; it just seems too unreal and too far removed from modern life.

But *Hamlet* is a play about the awakening of man. The real you, your *Higher Self** can receive its inner message directly.

What is this, the Higher Self? It is what you experience if you pay attention to this present moment only, without letting any thoughts come in. But it is so delicate, rapid and fleeting that in our usual dull state – occupied with the concern of the day – it is almost unnoticeable.

So, you must above all be open and *present** to this

---

1 Esoteric terms with specific meanings are printed in Italics the first time they are used and, if they carry a star (*), they are also fully described in the Glossary

play as you watch it – not analysing it, or letting thoughts or associations take attention away from it; simply letting it flow over you like gentle waves on the sea shore, being aware of it and its effect on you. Whoever really wishes to grasp the total meaning of *Hamlet*, can bring this kind of openness to it and indeed Shakespeare evokes it several times in the play by having various bizarre events happen. These are the anomalies, or what we shall call *shocks** in Shakespeare's play.

The course of the play shows a soul passing through events that lead from sleep to awakening, finally reaching a full awareness. The play is in fact all about one single individual. His soul is portrayed by Hamlet himself, and all the characters in the play represent parts of the psychology of this individual such as his inner confusion; his emotional needs; his *false personality** (the 'self' he shows to people he wants to impress); his serious thinking side (his principles and what he understands about life – what we are going to call his *true personality**); and so on; and they all affect the soul in their own ways. All the actions in the play are internal psychological events taking place inside the person who is awakening.

However, Shakespeare's art is so sublime that there is something in *Hamlet* for everybody. It is an example of *objective art** – art that initially strikes everybody the same way but leaves them with a thousand thoughts.

Objective Art can always be recognised by its initial momentary impact: that it is somehow mysterious and full of meaning. Almost immediately after, thinking takes over and everybody will have their own opinion about it. But it is that initial impact that counts. We have only to remember the first moment of seeing the great Pyramid of Giza or the Cathedral of Chartres actually standing before us, or of seeing the statue of the Hindu god Vishnu with six arms to know what objective art is. But our lower self jumps in and tries to find explanations. There are so many dimensions, aspects and details in objective art that one is apt to become engrossed in them and forget the original impact.

Hamlet contains meaning at many levels of understanding. It is after all a play to be performed for the general public. Everyone can take something from it yet remain intrigued by its incongruities. It expresses a living truth in a vehicle that has been preserved since it was written, four hundred years ago. Its message cannot be destroyed by changes of language (it has been translated into nearly eighty languages), or by personal tastes of directors. Even if it is badly performed the message is still there and it is a supreme example of a form carrying the message that I described in the first chapter.

Basically *Hamlet* contains two main messages: the first is that you cannot awaken just by behaving differently from now on, that is by "adding virtue", because your old self will absorb the new and make it its own, thus corrupting it. Shakespeare has Hamlet say it this way:

> *Virtue cannot so inoculate our old stock but we shall relish of it*   (III, 1,117)

Consequently, you have to remove the *old stock* completely – your entire *old self* has to go.

The second message is that: in order to completely remove the old self you must even remove the part *which is doing the removing*.

In *Hamlet* the removal of a psychological part is portrayed by the death of a character. This clears up one of the most perplexing questions about *Hamlet*, namely, why are there so many deaths and why do most of the characters die at the end?

Try to see these characters as parts of yourself. Insofar as you have understood a character, or the course of action a character takes, you already have that in yourself. I shall be constantly switching back and fore between the characters in the play and their inner psychological meanings in you. In most places where I need to refer to the awakening human being (rather than to Hamlet himself), I shall refer to "you" to avoid otherwise cumbersome text.

CHAPTER 3
The Play Begins

'Hamlet' is your sensed need to awaken, represented by the main character of the play. It begins as a sense that something is wrong with your life and a longing to see reality. As the play progresses this element gathers strength and substance. But in the beginning it is undeveloped and entirely unable to control the processes that go on in the other areas of your psychology. All these areas are represented by the other characters in the play, and their actions in the play represent workings that take place inside you. We can say that in the beginning 'Hamlet' is just your *magnetic centre**.

By Act V however, 'Hamlet' has become a fully-fledged soul and has a certain identity. So we can speak of it as "he". He is ready to give up everything for his quest – even himself. A more accurate way to say it is that he has become *Steward** (that is, your 'ruling faculty', which can control all your other psychological features). He does however die intentionally (we shall see later how his death is intentional), and for something other than himself – the *Higher Self*.

The play takes place in the land of Denmark,

which symbolises the inner psychological world of the awakening soul. The actions happen in and around the castle at Elsinore, which represents the whole being, the sum total of who you are.

London audiences in Shakespeare's time would have regarded Denmark as somewhat distant and harsh, home of many savage Viking invasions of past history that had left a mark on the British psyche. They would therefore have believed quite readily that there were strange goings-on there.

On the other hand, England was their everyday experience, and so in the play England represents the humdrum struggles of daily life. When Hamlet is sent to England in Act IV to be executed, it means that your wish to awaken is being subjected to life-experiences to destroy its will.

And so at the beginning of the play, we find Prince Hamlet in an unhappy condition, as in the words:

> *Something is rotten in the state of Denmark*
>
> *(I,4,90)*

Shakespeare is saying here that something is rotten in your psychological world. The soul is still dormant and things are not right.

We could hardly blame Hamlet for being confused, morose and angry. He is the son of the dead King of Denmark, a man who had been admired and revered by everyone, and loved by his wife the Queen Gertrude. But the King died in mysterious

The Awakening of Man

Elsinore Castle

circumstances and in less than a month, Gertrude married his brother, Claudius, who has now become the new King. Already something is very wrong here, not to say bizarre. The new king is Hamlet's uncle; his mother, Gertrude simply forgets her erstwhile husband and marries his brother!

We should not, by the way, overlook the meanings of family relationships. For example, Hamlet is Gertrude's son, and she represents the emotional centre, which means that the wish to awaken is born from the emotional centre. However, Gertrude is weak and we shall come back to her. Also, Hamlet of course is the son of his dead father – he is his heir 'by blood', so he has a fundamental birthright. This is made very clear because his father had the same name and was known as King Hamlet.

But even before we see Hamlet himself, Shakespeare shows us the ghost of his dead father appearing to some watchmen in the castle, and then to Horatio, Hamlet's bosom friend.

The Ghost of Hamlet's father represents the original true state of man, which lies buried ('killed') by the time of adulthood. In a child, its appearance is belittled or, more usually, ignored by parents and thereafter it is constantly suppressed. It exists in an adult as *conscience** (a sense of strictly personal right and wrong over and above socially accepted morals) - little more than a wisp of its former sense - and does not manifest often, being usually a prompting of something you know you ought to do, or not do, in the moment.

Shakespeare portrays this by having the ghost appear at night, in other words the person in whom it appears is asleep in the esoteric sense. The watchmen who see him are simply some *I's** (thoughts, impulses and feelings). They are afraid and they call upon Horatio to join them.

Horatio plays an important role in the rest of the play, as we shall see, taking on the part of narrator at some points, of confidant to Hamlet at others, and always supporting him in his endeavours. He is a solid consistent friend, he does not believe in whims or supernatural explanations, and clearly recognises the truth, even if he does not understand it.

Horatio often acts as a kind of *deputy steward** (having less authority than *Steward*), knowing the background of Hamlet's plight and trying to put things in order, with or without Hamlet. At one point it is clear that Horatio does not completely comprehend all that is going on because Hamlet says to him:

> *There are more things in heaven and earth Horatio*
> *Than are dreamt of in your philosophy*
> (I,5,166)

Later we shall see that Horatio finally develops into that which we call the *nine-of-hearts** (the element in your emotional centre that reveres the

Higher Self). This is an aspect where Shakespeare has combined two roles.

And so it is that Horatio knows that the watchmen really have seen something because he finally sees it himself and instantly recognises it as Hamlet's father. But he senses that it will only speak to Hamlet, and that only Hamlet can deal with it.

This way the audience will know later that the ghost is not just a figment of Hamlet's imagination (who can be considered as subject to hallucination, since he seems to be quite mad at the beginning,). And so it means that the ghost is real for us too.

But Shakespeare does not show us Hamlet yet. He first introduces the other main characters of the play. From one angle he is keeping us in suspense because Hamlet is the protagonist.

But the inner meaning of this is that the awakening element: 'Hamlet' in you is just not around much at the beginning – the whole of your inner world is occupied by other concerns (characters in the play). That is why there is something rotten in the state of Denmark. Only Horatio is around, who at this stage can be regarded as a group of *I's** that can recognise something higher but can do little about it.

CHAPTER 4
Hamlet's Other Counterparts

We are in the court at the castle of Elsinore, which if you remember, represents the whole of your psychology. Shakespeare now introduces the four main characters that will, sooner or later, be psychological obstacles to awakening.

During the festive ceremony to celebrate the marriage of the new King to Gertrude, Claudius the king makes a speech saying that the sadness of his brother's death can be balanced by the happiness of his marriage to Gertrude and the court should now all rejoice – a typical ruse to cover up uncomfortable facts by bringing in agreeable distractions.

Claudius is the main antagonist in this play and clearly represents the lower self. He is devious, calculating and manipulative, taking an innocent position whenever he is visible, but always working schemes behind the scenes when he is not. He is indeed far ahead of all the others, having achieved his plans well before anyone even notices that there were any plans.

In particular he marries Gertrude even before Hamlet realises there is anything wrong at all.

And of course Hamlet blames Gertrude for it, as her guilt is palpable. Although we shall see that Gertrude is quite weak, it is in fact Claudius who is the villain and causes all the other characters to play their parts in his schemes without their knowing his true motives. This is just like the snake in the myth of the garden of Eden, who tempts Eve first. Shakespeare is well aware of this as he portrays the murder as taking place in a garden and he even alludes to the very first murder of brother by brother.

In the same way, if you are starting to awaken, your lower self manipulates your I's in the background and you blame yourself for things you think or do that are actually the results of his guile, and you forget about awakening – which is his goal.

Claudius then calls upon Laertes to speak at the court. Laertes is a young nobleman who has returned from France to be at the coronation of Claudius. Laertes declares that he wishes to go back to France to further pursue his career (and seek his fortune), and asks his father, who is also at the ceremony, for permission to do so.

Laertes represents the definite, 'professional' part of your psychology, and we shall see more of him. Laertes is completely turned to Life. He is earnest and whole-hearted, but he is also passionate and competitive. His ambitions are represented by France (professional life).

When the play was first performed, Frenchmen were a common sight in London. London was a refuge for the French Huguenots who were being persecuted by Catholics in France. They were mostly well educated and earnest but also rather passionate about their cause. Shakespeare could then readily use France for Laertes' somewhat headstrong character.

Later we shall see that Laertes also represents worldly wisdom as distinct from any spiritual understanding. With all these aspects he represents your practical side, or what we can call *true personality**.This will be expanded later.

His father speaks next and gives him permission to leave for France. This is Polonius, who is the Lord Chamberlain, and thus he is an important man in the court – and he knows it.

Polonius is a character providing a lighter relief from the heavy melancholy of the play. Polonius exhibits much pomp, vanity and pride. He is fussy, has an opinion about everything and is somewhat superficial. Thus we may say that he represents *false personality**.

Note that Laertes is the son of Polonius and so is intimately related to him in your psychology. Both are turned outward to deal with life on different scales — Laertes more intentionally than Polonius.

Finally Claudius turns to Hamlet and asks why he still grieves - every son mourned a father, he says, but to continue so long is being stubborn. He says he can regard him, Claudius, as his new father, and when he dies, Hamlet shall succeed him. All his words are so clearly disingenuous that most of the audience will see them so, particularly as it is most obvious that had Claudius not taken over the throne, it would have fallen to Hamlet directly. Here, the lower self has usurped the status and power reserved for the awakened soul.

Hamlet asks to return to University where he was studying before the coronation, but Claudius does not wish it. The lower self does not wish the *magnetic centre** to further educate itself (about awakening), as that would be a threat to its existence.

Hamlet is reluctant. But since his mother Gertrude also wishes him to stay close to her, he complies.

Gertrude represents a vulnerable undeveloped emotional centre, easily affected by life's disappointments. In most men emotional reactions are repressed or not understood, rather than accommodated and handled maturely. The emotional centre left to itself constantly seeks reassurance – support and love, or admiration and acceptance. These are aspects which underlie *feminine dominance**. Gertrude rapidly reacted to the loss of her husband by finding another. And of course Claudius (the lower self) stepped in and fulfilled that role, as was his intention all along. So we see the emotional centre under the will of the lower self – a common feature in man and woman. We have now seen four main characters preventing awakening. There is one more, Ophelia, which we shall see soon.

The Awakening of Man

Queen Gertrude

CHAPTER 5
Hamlet Rejects the World

The King and Queen leave the court with all the courtiers, and Hamlet is left alone, morose, feeling an utter disgust with his life and his world, considering suicide and wishing he could just disappear:

> *Oh that this too solid flesh would melt,*
> *Thaw and resolve itself into a dew.*
> (I,2,129)

He rants against the world, calling it an *unweeded garden that grows to seed*. The 'world' here is of course your inner psychological world which Hamlet sees is like an untended garden left to grow weeds. This is the desperation you feel at the beginning when you start to see how your life and your character has turned out, that it is filled with meaningless drives and obligations, that it is going nowhere, and it seems you cannot change it.

Hamlet decries his mother who used to cling to his father, yet less than a month after his death, married Claudius. He says:

> *Frailty, thy name is woman* (I,2,146)

Commentators often assume this means that women are weak and fickle. But in fact, Hamlet

Hamlet – Henry Irving 1888

is saying that the weak part of your psychology is the emotional centre. It needs to be guided by reason, that is, it needs cultivation by a 'husband', to weed out its prejudices and indulgences. Ideally this would be your *Steward* (which, as I have said, would be your 'ruling faculty' that can control all your other psychological features). But at this point in the play Hamlet is too weak to be the steward, not to mention that his uncle is unfit to be a good husband such as his father was. He says this clearly:

> *My father's brother, no more like my father than I to Hercules.* (I,2,152)

In general then, Hamlet is seeing the seriousness of his situation and all the things that are wrong and need to be put right. The famous mystic G. I. Gurdjieff once referred to this as "the Terror of the Situation". Who, that ever started to awaken, has not been in this state?

But he still does not know how his father died (how the Higher Self disappeared). He suspects Claudius had something to do with it and as the play goes on he becomes more certain.

By this time Hamlet's friend Horatio has already encountered the ghost of Hamlet's father. But the ghost would not speak to him. Horatio tells Hamlet about it. When Hamlet asks him if he is sure of what he is talking about he says:

I knew your father:
These hands are not more like. (I,2,211)

In modern English parlance, that is: "I know him like the back of my hand". So we see that Horatio is familiar with what is higher, just as deputy steward knows what is higher, if only indirectly – the ghost does not speak to him. But at this stage there is precious little *being** to deal with it.

CHAPTER 6
Worldly Wisdom and Young Naivety

Shakespeare now introduces the other main character of the play, Ophelia, the sister of Laertes and daughter of Polonius. We might say she is the 'love interest' in the play, but there is precious little love actually seen. However, it is clear that she is already involved with Hamlet when Laertes speaks to her. She is a passive young woman, hardly more than a girl, who accepts without question whatever her brother tells her.

Ophelia represents undeveloped *Essence** as in a little child: innocent, naïve, sensitive, and lacking in discrimination. Having not been exposed to raw life, it accepts everything at face value. In most people essence remains in this form their entire lives, being buried deep within (false) personality.

Laertes warns Ophelia about Hamlet. He tells her that Hamlet's love for her can so easily change:

> *Forward, not permanent, sweet, not lasting*
> (I,3,8)

Basically he says that Hamlet cannot be trusted.

We can see here how personality (your reasoning

part) tries to protect essence (your sensitive, vulnerable part) from some new element in your life of which you are not yet sure, and does not fit with your established way of looking at things. This is only to be expected since that is what personality is for.

Polonius comes to wish his son good passage, and urges him to hurry up as the ship is waiting to leave.

Nevertheless he spends a long time giving Laertes a lengthy list of things to remember on how to conduct his future life. He actually gives Laertes some very good advice, which he has picked up somewhere, and Laertes takes it to heart.

The salient things he says are:

> *Give thy thoughts no tongue,*
> *Nor any unproportion'd thought his act.*
> *[…]*
> *Beware of entrance to a quarrel; but, being in,*
> *Bear't that the opposed may beware of thee.*
>
> *Give every man thine ear, but few thy voice:*
> *Take each man's censure, but reserve thy judgment.*
> *[…]*
> *Neither a borrower nor a lender be:*
> *For loan oft loses both itself and friend;*
> *And borrowing dulls the edge of husbandry.*

This above all,–to thine own self be true;
And it must follow, as the night the day,
Thou canst not then be false to any man
(I,3,59)

This advice is good and at this stage of awakening it represents the best of values useful for your life – a step which is still not so esoteric. Also, by using this device, Shakespeare explicitly shows us the principles that Laertes takes on and lives by.

Laertes leaves and Polonius turns to Ophelia. On hearing of her conversation with Laertes, he more or less repeats what Laertes said to her about avoiding being hurt by Hamlet – of course speaking in his own way with many words and sense of urgency.

We have now met all the major characters of the play except one, their roles in Hamlet's life, and in awakening. Some of them still need to emerge as full characters. The remaining figure will appear at the end of the play, although he is mentioned at various times. We shall deal with him later.

The Awakening of Man

Hamlet and the ghost of his father

CHAPTER 7
Hamlet Meets the Ghost

The next night Hamlet climbs the stairs to the castle ramparts with Horatio, where he had encountered the ghost. Notice that 'climbing up' denotes reaching for higher parts and this is Hamlet's first effort. Also, he is reaching in the dark.

The ghost appears once again and Horatio leaves. Now it speaks to Hamlet. It tells him that while the King was taking his afternoon nap in his garden, Claudius murdered him by pouring lethal poison into his ear (symbolising that hearing poisonous words from the lower self 'kills' man's higher parts). He tells him that his death must be avenged. But, he says that Hamlet is not to harm his mother Gertrude:

> *Nor let thy soul contrive against thy mother*
> *aught. Leave her to heaven* (I,5,86)

In other words do not punish your emotional part for being weak and insubstantial. It is not the culprit. It will of itself become more aware of the truth.

The Ghost's famous final words to Hamlet are:

> *Remember me* (I,5,91)

This is quite clearly *Remember Yourself*.

All this deeply affects Hamlet. He has seen his dead father! In the heat of the moment he decides to give up all his worldly learning and dedicate himself to avenging him. But he does not yet know how much anguish and strife that will cause him, which we shall see in the rest of the play.

This is like your first taste of something higher and real within you, such as: when you encounter someone who causes you to see your whole self in a fresh new light; or you meet an esoteric school; or simply when in unusual circumstances a very personal experience reveals a deep cosmic truth to you. You awaken for a split second. It is so definite yet strange that you decide you will give up everything worldly and concentrate on getting it again – a commendable aim, though somewhat naïve, since you don't know what you are letting yourself in for.

Hamlet is clearly upset by this encounter. He was already disconsolate before he met the ghost but now the ghost has revealed to him how he died at the hands of Claudius, something which caused Hamlet to blurt out: *Oh my prophetic soul!*, meaning that he had already feared it in his heart.

He vows to avenge his father but is confronted with the prospect of dealing with Claudius – a ruthless, powerful and potentially fierce man. Claudius would undoubtedly have him killed, and Hamlet still cannot trust any of the others. He forces Horatio and the watchmen to swear never to reveal the encounter with the Ghost. From then on he hides his discovery behind a mask of madness. This is not too difficult because he is already somewhat unbalanced by all the goings on and only has to exaggerate it.

Shakespeare is showing here that Hamlet still believes that the other characters are real. Hamlet is still weak and his only weapon at this point is a feigned madness. But he has been given the first indication that things are not what they seem.

This equates to the uncertain situation you find yourself in when you have decided to try to awaken, but you don't quite want to give up all your values and conclusions about life yet – because they might be real after all. It is somewhat like a child who, though he has found out that Santa Claus does not exist, still goes along with all the antics, just in case he's wrong.

How to proceed with awakening? Somehow you have to pretend to yourself that you won't change anything really – that you are only experimenting (just like Hamlet feigning madness when he is already a bit mad). In the Bible, Christ refers to this as not letting the left hand know what the right hand is doing. This is pretty easy in the beginning because most parts of you don't want to change anyway!

But this internal feigning of madness is useful at later stages too. That is why whenever you are working towards *conscious presence**, you must not let expectations creep in, for as soon as you do that you tip off the lower self (Claudius).

We have now come to the end of the first Act in the play. All the characters have been introduced, and some of them already show their colours. We also know the general thrust of the Play because Hamlet has been charged with avenging the death of his father. And we know that the culprit is Claudius, but we don't know how Hamlet is going to deal with him. We only know that Hamlet doesn't seem to know what he is doing and that there will be lots of deaths. It doesn't sound too good for Hamlet. But remember that Shakespeare has a message here, and things are not what they seem.

CHAPTER 8
The First Impediments

The next act starts with a scene that gives a fuller picture of Polonius and Ophelia, and Hamlet's relationship to her. We shall see how Polonius and Ophelia are basic hindrances to awakening (in two entirely different ways), and you will have to deal with them before making any further progress.

First, Polonius sends a helper to spy on Laertes in France to check that he is behaving properly. He explains to him in minute detail how to ask people questions about Laertes and how not to spoil his son's reputation with them.

It represents *inner considering** (worrying about what other people are thinking), a mark of false personality.

Ophelia appears; she is still upset after having been accosted by Hamlet who was in a dishevelled state, wearing dirty and loose clothes, grabbing her wrist tightly, and peering intently into her face. Maybe he is really a little bit mad after all? Anyway Polonius assumes he is madly in love with her and makes way to tell King Claudius.

This scene shows something of the character of Ophelia – how obedient she is, naïve and innocent, in fact *non-existent** (a trait in which one lives through other people's whims and decisions, and does not decide anything for oneself).

But for you, the awakening person, it represents (in most people) the dispirited nature of an *essence* that has never been allowed to express itself and thus gain individuality. It is totally under the rule of either false personality (Polonius), or of decisions made in your profession (represented by Laertes), which false personality (Polonius) still fusses over.

As for Hamlet, what does he represent here? Your soul is starting to awaken; it is starting to examine your own nature. Hamlet already knows false personality – as we shall see later – but essence is still a mystery to him since it was so hidden. Hence the 'peering intently' at it. That Hamlet's clothes are untidy and his actions clumsy merely shows the artless nature of a budding soul not yet aware of itself.

In the next scene Shakespeare introduces two lesser though still significant hindrances. Claudius calls two nobles into his presence, Rosencrantz and Guildenstern, who have been studying at the same university as Hamlet. He asks them to check on Hamlet, to cheer him up and find out what is troubling him.

Although he feigns concern about Hamlet's welfare, his real aim is to find out how much of a threat Hamlet is to him.

However, Rosencrantz and Guildenstern are not aware of that. They are not very bright; they are superficial; and they are so eager to be in the King's favour that they are easily fooled. Hamlet never takes them seriously. Indeed, Shakespeare portrays them as bumbling and foolish.

Claudius engaging these two represents the lower self looking for a way to divert your soul from its journey of self-discovery. And to do this it attempts to engage interests that the magnetic centre previously had (represented by Hamlet's studies at the university).

Rosencrantz and Guildenstern leave. At this point Polonius announces the return of two ambassadors who had been sent to Norway and they appear before the King.

They report on Prince Fortinbras, son of the dead Norwegian King who Hamlet's father had conquered in the past (his name was also Fortinbras, just as Hamlet's father's name was also Hamlet – the significance of this will be seen later). Prince Fortinbras had sought to attack Denmark but after some diplomacy now will no longer attack Denmark but wishes safe passage through the country to attack Poland.

In the context of the play this change is entirely incomprehensible. Instead of invading a country the prince now wishes to pass through it peaceably to attack another!

It is one of the *shocks* Shakespeare uses to shake up the audience, and alert anyone more awake that here is more than meets the eye. It has a point which will become clear later, but on the face of it, it seems to be utterly nonsensical. We will leave it for the moment with just the words: do not let the left hand know what the right hand is doing.

The ambassadors leave and Polonius tells the king and queen about Hamlet's love for his daughter Ophelia. He shows them a letter which Hamlet wrote to her. This contains, amongst others, the famous words:

> *Doubt thou the stars are fire;*
> *Doubt that the sun doth move;*
> *Doubt truth to be a liar;*
> *But never doubt I love.*
> (II,2,115)

Then comes one of Polonius' long drawn out speeches in which he tells them that after Ophelia had rejected him, Hamlet fell into madness. The king and queen, not convinced the madness is connected with Hamlet's love, agree on advice from Polonius, to watch an encounter between Hamlet and Ophelia which Polonius will set up for them.

They see Hamlet coming and Polonius approaches him.

He speaks to him but Hamlet claims he doesn't know him, calling him a "fishmonger". This is an insult but Polonius doesn't see it as he already assumes Hamlet is mad. The words Hamlet uses leave the audience in no doubt what he thinks of Polonius. And indeed, your growing soul would indeed find your false personality tiresome. However, Polonius does notice something in Hamlet's ravings, saying:

> *Though this be madness, yet there is method in't* (II,2,202)

This is a signal to us from Shakespeare that things which seem weird on the face of it, have an inner meaning. He is telling us here to look for the *method in't* – not just here but in the whole of the play.

In any case Polonius leaves, bent on setting up the meeting between Hamlet and Ophelia.

Rosencrantz and Guildenstern now return and start inquiring after Hamlet's well-being. There follows a lot of banter. At one point Hamlet asks them (paraphrased): *what have you done that fortune has sent you to prison?* (He is saying their blind devotion to the king – the inscrutable lower self – is their prison. But here is a deeper meaning alluding to limitations of certain well-known secret societies. See Appendix A).

When the two obviously don't understand what he is talking about, he retorts: *Denmark's a prison* which means the psychological world surrounding the awakening soul, that is to say Hamlet's world in the play, or your own inner world, is a prison.

Both of his statements about prison are true but on different scales.

Rosencrantz answers that he does not think Denmark is a prison (taking the point literally). And Hamlet replies that that is fine for Rosencrantz because:

> *There is nothing good or bad but thinking*
>
> *makes it so.* (II,2,245)

The usual way of taking this line is that the way we look at things makes them good or bad. And that is true but it is yet more profound: if you never see your life as a prison, it will be fine and dandy for you, but you will never try to awaken.

Hamlet then asks them why they have come, although he already knows and says so. After a lot of fumbling and clumsy attempts to hide their mission they finally admit that the king and queen sent them to him.

Hamlet therefore explains to them his melancholy and that they can just tell the king and queen that he is mad sometimes and not others. He continues that, although Man can be a wonderful creature, it doesn't delight him:

What a piece of work is a man, how noble in reason, how infinite in faculties, in form and moving how express and admirable, in action how like an angel, in apprehension how like a god […] and yet to me what is this quintessence of dust? Man delights not me
[II,2,299]

It is here that Shakespeare lays bare the fundamental irony of awakening. A true Man is all these things, but an ordinary everyday man is only an imitation of them. He has lost, or never had, their original conscious nature and is thus no more than a *quintessence of dust* (a raw origin of dust), such that he *delights not*.

But Rosencrantz of course misses the point and tells Hamlet that the imminent arrival of a troupe of stage-players might cheer him up from this melancholy he has.

The actors arrive, and a merry band they are. Hamlet requests the lead actor to give him a special performance on the spot. It is a speech from a play about Troy and the actor performs it with great drama and very convincing emotion.

Hamlet is amazed at how the actor can play something so well that was clearly not his emotional state at the moment of asking. He has an idea – he asks them to put on a play the next day, "The Murder of Gonzago", a play they know and which portrays the murder of a King in a garden. Hamlet asks them to make a little addition he has thought up. He intends with this to show exactly how his father died and with that, to watch the reactions of Claudius.

After asking Polonius to take care of the well-keeping of the actors, Hamlet is left alone on the stage.

He marvels that a mere actor can generate such wealth of emotion and meaning for some character that is nothing more than a simple invention in a play. If only he could present himself like that to Claudius?

Hamlet can see here that *the I's are not real** (the emotions of the actor are patently artificial), yet they can be very convincing. You believe your own I's even though they are nothing more than electrical discharges in your brain. Hamlet is still fascinated by the engaging reality of them yet he still does not completely believe the ghost of his father – he still wonders if it may have been an apparition and that is why he wishes to test Claudius – but also test the ghost.

Likewise, you do not yet have enough confidence in what the Higher Self, your metaphysical self, has whispered to you (it does not make dramatic acts), so you search for proof.

He frets that he cannot confront Claudius in any other way than by words and plays. He feels himself too weak. And indeed Hamlet is still a weak soul at this juncture. He still has to deal with Ophelia (though he does not know it) and with Polonius, who are both still burdening him – the one, Polonius, is false personality that weighs him down with its fussiness and attention to how it looks to others; the other, Ophelia, is tender essence that, such as it is, cannot offer any support.

But he tells himself that if Claudius so much as

blenches (pales) at the play then he will know that he is guilty, and will know what to do. He ends by saying:

> *The play's the thing*
> *Wherein I'll catch the conscience of the king.*
> (II,2,591)

This has a second meaning for, as well as Hamlet catching the conscience of Claudius with his play, the entire play of *Hamlet* is where Shakespeare will catch the conscience of you – or more specifically, your lower self.

We now know all the characters and their roles in Hamlet's play. In a sense the play hasn't really started. Shakespeare has only been laying out the pieces on the board.

But now we can begin.

CHAPTER 9
Hamlet Shows His Hand

The king and queen are at court with Polonius, Rosencrantz and Guildenstern. Ophelia also comes in.

Rosencrantz and Guildenstern make a report to the king and queen, that they can find no cause for Hamlet's madness. Though he seemed aloof he answered their questions well. He was however pleased to see the actors who had just arrived. Claudius thus asks them to proceed with the preparations for the play and they leave. He also asks Gertrude to leave since he wishes for Hamlet to meet Ophelia alone, as if by accident.

Claudius and Polonius prepare to watch the coming encounter between Hamlet and Ophelia. Polonius asks her to go out of sight for now, but to enter later reading a religious book.

Hamlet enters.

He is heavy with doubt and indecision. He has seen some I's that seemed real but weren't (the performance of the actor); he has encountered an inner state that did not seem so real (the ghost) which urged him to avenge it, but he is not sure about it because he has no identity yet. He cannot go forward – he has no strength to deal with these I's – but he cannot go back – he has already seen too much. He is alone and full of dread. It is a period of real suffering. He now speaks what must be the best known words of Shakespeare:

> *To be, or not to be: that is the question.*
> *Whether 'tis nobler in the mind to suffer*
> *The slings and arrows of outrageous fortune*
> *Or to take arms against a sea of troubles,*
> *And by opposing end them*
> (III,1,56)

In anguish he exclaims it would be better to die, except that what awaits him after death could be even worse than life! And *"there's the Rub"*, he moans, because:

> *the dread of something after death,–*
> *The undiscover'd country, from whose bourn*
> *No traveller returns,–puzzles the will,*
> *And makes us rather bear those ills we have*
> *Than fly to others that we know not of?*
> *Thus conscience does make cowards of us all;*
> *[…] And lose the name of action.*
> (III,1,78)

So much has been written about this that it hardly bears more interpretation. Yet we can realise one thing: whenever there is strife for something you deeply and honestly want involving un-guessable hazards and dangers, you go through a phase like this. It is the final time before you take the decision that you know you have to take in spite of any risks. It is the darkest moment, the moment before the dawn, the dark night of the soul.

For Hamlet it is nothing less than giving up his whole life for something far greater. He wants it but cannot define what it is. And so it is with awakening for all of us. A price has to be paid and that price is nothing less than giving up your entire 'life' – all your principles, your comforts, theories and indulgences, in other words who you think you are. The question is: are you prepared to pay everything or not? – *that is the question*.

At this fraught point Ophelia walks in reading the book. She greets Hamlet and gives him back some gifts he gave her, saying:

> *Rich gifts wax poor when givers prove*
> *unkind.* (III,1,101)

That is, his former declarations of love for her were false. She completely misses his state of anguish, just as a child would not notice its parents' worries.

Ophelia faces Hamlet

But in this state of torment Hamlet tells her he never loved her and he starts to taunt her:

> *Are you honest?*
>
> *Are you fair [beautiful]?*
>
> *If you be honest and fair, your honesty should admit no discourse to your beauty.*
> (III,1,103)

In other words, if you are honest as well as beautiful, your honesty should not allow any pandering at all to your beauty.

> *For the power of beauty will sooner transform honesty from what it is into a bawd than the force of honesty can translate beauty into his likeness.*
> (III,1,111)

Beauty, not itself a virtue, overcomes honesty for its own self-aggrandizement (indicated by *bawd* – a person who supplies prostitutes), but honesty has little power to assimilate beauty. Here he also says the words already quoted in the chapter *The Art of Shakespeare*:

> *Virtue cannot so inoculate our old stock but we shall relish of it*
> (III, 1,117)

By confronting your essence like this, your soul examines your true inner nature (your 'Ophelia'), and sees that although it has the beauty and cuteness of a child, there is little or no honesty. A child is not naturally virtuous; it has no understanding of values, of right and wrong, and has no will or strength. It needs to be schooled in values, honesty and nobility.

This is what Hamlet says in the next exchange about going to a nunnery, which at first seems to be pure nastiness and a bitter denunciation of women. But it is in fact a sincere observation of the weak inner nature of all of us. Remember that Shakespeare has already given us the key to this by saying: *"Frailty thy name is woman"*. So whenever Hamlet alludes to *woman* he is actually talking about the inner weakness of both man and woman, especially one who wishes to awaken.

> *Get thee to a Nunnery.*
> *Why wouldst thou be a breeder of sinners?*

(III,1,121)

Sinners here are frivolous or aimless thoughts (originally, the verb to sin meant to miss the mark). Hamlet continues his diatribe by explicitly including himself:

> *I am myself indifferent honest; but yet I could accuse me of such things that it were better my mother had not borne me:*
> *I am very proud, revengeful, ambitious; with more offences at my beck than I have thoughts to put them in, imagination to give them shape, or time to act them in.*
> (III,1,122)

Hamlet is beginning to observe himself more, and all 'men' (all I's):

> *We are arrant knaves all: believe none of us.*
> (III,1,128)

Claudius and Polonius have been watching the whole scene, and now Claudius gets worried for the first time – Hamlet is seeing too much – he is observing too many things that Claudius prefers to keep hidden. He says that Hamlet's behaviour did not seem like love to him but something more sinister. He decides that Hamlet should be sent to England, noting to Polonius that the sea voyage and experience of a different country will clear up his condition.

I have already mentioned that England represents daily life and its hum-drum activities. Claudius is going to send Hamlet there, thus to smother his quest. Furthermore, he explicitly mentions the sea voyage - a treacherous endeavour. We can equate the sea to *imagination** - (esoterically, the endless waves of thoughts and images coming from all directions). What better way for your lower self to smother any intent to awaken?

CHAPTER 10
Hamlet's First Achievement

The court gathers in order to watch the play within a play. But also, Hamlet intends to watch the reactions of Claudius, and tells Horatio to be alert.

Hamlet sits next to Ophelia and makes suggestive remarks to her of a vaguely sexual nature. This is not surprising if you remember that your soul and essence are intimately close to each other. But it also serves to divert any suspicion that Claudius may have had about Hamlet's true intentions.

The play re-enacts the story of Gonzago Duke of Vienna, and his wife Baptista. As it starts they are strolling in a garden and talking. He tells her he may not be with her much longer in this life, and that she ought to take a new husband when he is gone. But she insists she will never take a second husband:

> *In second husband let me be accurst!*
> *None wed the second but who killed the first.*
> (III,2,170)

- a clear pointer to the current situation. Her husband warns her that her strong reaction is only fleeting and will at some time subside, saying:

What to ourselves in passion we propose,
The passion ending, doth the purpose lose.
(III,2,185)

All these words are clearly an allusion to Gertrude and may well be what Hamlet asked the players to insert into the play. Again here, Shakespeare is indicating the fickleness of the emotional centre (represented by Gertrude).

After a while Baptista leaves Gonzago in the garden and he takes a nap. While he is asleep his nephew, Lucianus creeps in, pours poison into his ear and then leaves.

Shortly after, Baptista returns and discovers her husband dead. The shock renders her distraught.

Lucianus returns and consoles her. At first she resists him, but slowly she comes round, and the murderer finally but rather quickly wins her love. They go off to be married.

At this point Claudius becomes so agitated that he stops the play before it is finished and he leaves the court, shouting:

Give me some light. Away! (III,2,258)

Now Hamlet is certain that Claudius is guilty.

Horatio agrees–Claudius was clearly alarmed at the moment the poison was poured into the king's ear. Hamlet is gleeful at the success of his ruse. He calls for music.

Gertrude, who was also disturbed by the play and

left with Claudius, sends an angry summons to Hamlet to meet her in her room. He prepares for the encounter, telling himself to be firm (*"speak daggers to her"*) but not to harm her physically.

Meanwhile Claudius calls on Rosencrantz and Guildenstern to prepare for the sea journey to England, taking Hamlet with them. He says clearly that Hamlet threatens his position, but they hardly seem to notice, hastening to agree with everything.

The lower self is rattled; it has been detected; it must scheme and plot to preserve its ascendancy.

They leave Claudius with Polonius, who offers to secrete himself in the queen's room and eavesdrop on the impending confrontation with Hamlet, no doubt wanting to get the news first. False personality loves being first with the news.

Let us pause for the moment, recap the situation and also preview a little what is soon to happen. Hamlet, your aim to awaken, has sprung a trap to catch your lower self – to photograph it in its actions – by recalling a memory of an incident, re-running the sequence of events in your mind with as much verisimilitude as possible, and then stepping in with a pointing finger at the moment of truth (when you can see your true motives). It is a very uncomfortable moment and you may feel privately embarrassed or even disgusted by your behaviour at that time. It is something you don't wish to happen again (your motives are now clear!), and you feel guilty. So we can see how Claudius feels.

Of course, some other I's in you feel a little proud that you are self-disciplined enough to confront yourself like this, even though it is purely internal, and you can even imagine telling someone about it. So here we see how Polonius feels – eager to be the centre of attention telling others what he saw.

Your emotional centre has been truly shaken by the revelation that what at first seemed like something you were justified in doing (or so you convinced yourself at the time); now sees that your true nature is anything but noble. So we can also see how Gertrude feels before the encounter with Hamlet. It explains how she confronts him in the way she does.

Back to the play. Claudius is alone in his chamber. At this point he is very much aware of his guilt as murderer of his brother, and he refers to the first biblical crime of humanity, namely Cain's murder of Abel.

He tries to absolve himself from sin by prayer, but he cannot, since he still very much enjoys the rich trappings of kingship and doesn't want to change that. His prayers have no connection to his true urges. Uncomprehending, he expresses it thus:

> *My words fly up, my thoughts remain below:*
> *Words without thoughts never to heaven go.*
> (III,3,97)

Claudius tries to pray

The lower self – itself the accumulation of all its past doings – does not want to give up its status of being in control. Mere words of prayer are thus empty.

This is indeed the point of the play–you cannot cover over with prayers and good resolutions that condition which you yourself (the lower self) have been building up inside you for many years. You can only create (under the guidance of an awakened teacher), a new and separate thing which here is represented by Hamlet. The lower self is not that thing and never will be– it can itself only imitate what it admires, reject what it hates, or repeat what it has always done– but you cannot remove it, *without removing yourself as well*.

Hamlet finds the way in the end as we shall see later, but it is at the cost of his own death, which however has a deeper meaning. This situation is well known and is described in the parable of the weeds that grew in a field of good corn while "men were sleeping" (Matthew 12:24). When the servants ask the master if they should remove the weeds he tells them: "No – since by removing the weeds you might remove good corn also. Let both grow until the harvest." At that point it will be easy to separate the corn from the weeds (Hamlet will have grown stronger and his 'seed' – the Higher Self – can be saved).

Hamlet sees Claudius praying in his chamber and rashly decides to kill him, pulling his sword.

But he pauses: if he kills him now while praying, he might go to heaven, whereas Hamlet's father languishes in a state of limbo because he was murdered before he could ask for absolution.

Hamlet therefore returns his sword to its sheath. He does not want Claudius in heaven – it is like the weeds, because Hamlet is not ready yet. We know that Claudius is your lower self, and does not in fact exist as a human being. There is no place for the lower self in the state of *conscious presence**, a property of the Higher Self, represented by 'heaven' in the play.

In Gertrude's chamber Polonius tells her to be firm with Hamlet, and to tell him he has gone too far (this is false personality dictating to the emotional centre, as usual). Then Polonius hides himself behind a curtain and waits.

Hamlet enters and Gertrude starts to rebuke him, telling him he has offended his father, which makes Hamlet very angry and he replies that she has offended *his* father. Shocked, she asks him if he has forgotten who he is speaking to? He answers:

> *You are the queen, your husband's brother's wife,*
> *And – were it not so, you are my mother.*
> (III,4,15)

– a very succinct accusation of her crime which bears a second reading:

*You are the queen, your husband's brother's wife,
And – were it not so, you are my mother.*
(III,4,15)

She tries to get up and Hamlet restrains her physically. Thinking he is mad she fears for her life and calls out, whereupon Polonius, himself alarmed, calls loudly from behind the curtain for help from the guards. Hamlet, thinking it is the King stabs his dagger through the curtain.

Polonius dies.

Gertrude is aghast at the killing. But Hamlet reminds her that to murder a king and then marry his brother is an even worse crime. He lifts the curtain and discovers that it is Polonius.

At this point one would expect Hamlet to be dumbfounded by his mistake. But he is not at all dismayed. He only says:

Thou wretched, rash, intruding fool, farewell!
(III,4)

Once again, on the face of it Hamlet has behaved completely unexpectedly – another shock to the presumably well-behaved, law-abiding members of the audience. This is another anomaly which, as I mentioned in the chapter *Sacred Messages in Art*, shows there is something else going on besides the obvious appearances of the play.

Hamlet now tells his mother all he knows about how Claudius killed his father and how it explains his apparently bizarre behaviour. He presses her with two pictures of his dear father and of Claudius side by side so that she can see the difference in their noble outlooks, and he continues reproving her actions until finally she says:

> *O Hamlet speak no more.*
> *Thou turn'st mine eyes into my very soul,*
> *and there I see such black and grained spots*
> (III,4,88)

Her discomfiture already shows on her face and she cannot take any more. The ghost of Hamlet's father appears to him to remind him to treat her kindly but Gertrude does not see it. Deeply distressed by his words, she agrees to have no further conjugal company of the king.

Hamlet's final words are for the dead Polonius, who:

> *Is now most still, most secret and most grave,*
> *Who was in life a foolish, prating knave.*
> (III,4,214)

With this he leaves, dragging the dead Polonius behind him.

We have now come to a significant point in the play.

Here the awakening soul has reached a definite stage, where it has overcome false personality for the first time, represented by the death of Polonius. It is the first achievement. Awakening is still embryonic and somewhat haphazard (after all,

Polonius's death was an accident, though it had to happen sooner or later). Although it is portrayed once only in the play (even the play cannot bring Polonius back from the dead!), in you it would happen many times, until false personality is so weak that it ceases to be a serious handicap.

Hamlet now knows who the culprit is and he knows who his accomplices are.

CHAPTER 11
A Change of Being

Polonius's death hardens Claudius' resolve to send Hamlet away to England quickly. It is not lost on him that it could have been he himself who died (of course he spares no thought for the loss of Polonius). He calls on Rosencrantz and Guildenstern to make ready for the voyage and then summoning Hamlet, tells him in silky words that he is only going to England for his own good.

He has already arranged with Rosencrantz and Guildenstern to deliver a letter to the English Crown requesting that Hamlet be executed there. Thus we see that the lower self plots to have the awakening soul crushed by life experiences (represented by England, and indeed by the hazardous crossing over unpredictable seas). In the play this plot is used once only; in our lives, the lower self uses this ploy over and over again.

There follows a curious interlude before embarkation in which Hamlet encounters a Captain in the army of Prince Fortinbras, which has been given permission to pass through Denmark to Poland. The captain tells him that the land they shall fight over is not worth a dime (a "ducat" in his terms), yet many men will die to gain it.

Hamlet is awed by the resolve of Fortinbras to do what he intends, in spite of whatever costs. In our present day and age this would only be the callous decisions of a politician, but in Shakespeare's day, the sovereign of the land, who was Elizabeth I, was loved by her subjects (and thus the audience of the play at that time), and was regarded as truly having the interests of the state and her subjects at heart. So we should see Hamlet's awe in that light.

It is a factor which leads to his own change. Up to now Hamlet has been lacking in resolve (contrary to the lower self, which easily bases its actions on gratification and self-preservation). It shows him that to be clear and definite about what he really wants is an important factor in awakening, irrespective of social mores and expectations.

And indeed he recognises an irresolute man:

> *What is a man,*
> *If his chief good and market of his time*
> *Be but to sleep and feed?*
> (IV,4,33)

And further, goading himself to be more forthright:

> *Rightly to be great*
> *Is not to stir without great argument,*
> *But greatly to find quarrel in a straw*
> *When honour's at the stake.*
> (IV,4,53)

That is to say, be firm and single-minded once you have found your true (*great*) and honourable aim;

and resist robustly even the merest internal doubt (*a straw*).

He certainly needs this clarity of purpose during his voyage over the North Sea. Suspecting that Rosencrantz and Guildenstern are up to no good, he examines their goods on board ship one night and finds the letter they are carrying.

Cunningly (using a property normally reserved for the lower self), he replaces the letter with one of his own in which he asks the Crown to execute the two men instead, stamping the seal of it with the ring he has from his dead father -- to give the letter more credibility.

Then their ship is attacked by pirates and Hamlet needs his wits about him. They manage to fight off the pirate's ship while he springs aboard and they abandon him. At first he is held captive, but later convinces the pirates that if they return him to Denmark, he has the power to arrange their pardon.

We see from all this that Hamlet goes through quite a lot in which he has to be *present*, intelligent, and above all, active. The voyage at sea has an effect opposite to what Claudius intended. The exposure of your soul to turbulent events in your life gives it mettle – but only after you have decided definitely what you are trying to become, and you make brave efforts to actually *be* that in spite of external circumstances.

It is a significant stage in awakening. You are finally sure what you are aiming for. You were always aiming for it, but it was not definite before, and you were not sure what you were prepared to give up in getting it. It is your *fundamental personal aim**.

When Hamlet returns we shall see he is a changed being.

CHAPTER 12
Laertes Seeks Revenge; Ophelia Dies

While Hamlet is still at sea, things are still going on in the castle at Elsinore (which, you may remember, represents the whole sum of who you are).

Let us rephrase that sentence. Whilst your awakening part is absent (at sea) the rest of your psychology carries on anyway. But you have set the cat among the pigeons by clobbering your false personality. Now you don't know what to do any more since your ordinary way of dealing automatically with life is no longer valid for you. You have *killed Polonius*. This is an early stage of awakening.

No longer can you let false personality deal with daily matters while you privately indulge your personal childhood weaknesses. You *loved Ophelia* once, but now no more.

Not only that, but you have *shocked* your moral sense of right and wrong and how to behave correctly, originally given to you by *your mother Gertrude*.

To cap it all, you have *forewarned your worst inner enemy Claudius* of your intention to supersede both him and the rest of your psychology at Elsinore Castle (yourself).

You are in trouble my friend. You are at sea. Gurdjieff said: "Happy is he who has no soul; happy is he who has one – but woe to him who has one in gestation!"

On with the play. Ophelia is beyond distraction with the loss of her father and enters the court overcome with grief. When Gertrude tries to speak to her she is incoherent, and sings meaningless songs. She goes away and Claudius remarks:

Poor Ophelia,
divided from herself and her fair judgment
(IV,5,84)

Laertes arrives and storms into the king's presence demanding revenge, having been told of his father's death. Claudius explains carefully that it was not he but Hamlet who did the deed, and who should be rightly punished. But he sent him away, he says, because the people love him and they would have started an outcry had he penalised him. He expects more news soon (that Hamlet has been executed but he cannot say that, for it would show he already knows, and thus planned it).

Elsewhere in the castle Horatio receives two sailors that come to him with a letter. It is from Hamlet saying he is back in Denmark and it describes his exploits at sea with the Pirates. It asks that other

Ophelia

letters the sailors are carrying be given to the king. It also asks Horatio to meet him quickly at a place the sailors will show him, where Hamlet has much to tell him, particularly of Rosencrantz and Guildenstern.

Horatio sends a messenger to the king with the letters and then follows the sailors out.

Claudius and Laertes are still speaking together. Being satisfied that it was not Claudius who killed his father, Laertes has now calmed a little. As they speak, the messenger arrives with the letters. The king reads that Hamlet has returned alone to Denmark and will explain all when he arrives.

Claudius is taken aback and not a little confused, but Laertes is rather pleased. He can now personally confront Hamlet.

But Claudius swiftly recovers and takes advantage of this to cook up a plan. He suggests to Laertes that, since Hamlet has always been a little jealous of Laertes's prowess with sword fencing even though he is pretty good himself, a way to settle the situation is to have a sword duel. In order to persuade Laertes, Claudius flatters him with stories he has heard of Laertes' mastery with the sword.

The duel will be loaded in Laertes' favour. First, his sword will have a keen edge (such is not usually the case with fencing swords); second, it will be tipped with poison such that a mere scratch of the point will cause the poison to enter the body. Thirdly, to make sure, Claudius will prepare a goblet of wine laced with lethal poison. If then by heat of fighting they become thirsty, or Hamlet wins the match, he will be given the goblet to drink. In his revengeful state of mind, Laertes agrees to all this.

The plan has been struck. But now another shock comes because Gertrude enters and breaks news that Ophelia has died by drowning in the river. She fell in and sank under the weight of water in her robes, while still singing songs of flowers.

Laertes in renewed shock and holding back his tears, swears clear vengeance, then leaves to prepare himself.

It will be clear to the audience that the sword duel will be the climax of the play. But (they might think) why is Hamlet duelling with Laertes? Shouldn't it be Claudius? After all he is clearly the villain. Even more so, since Laertes gains nothing by winning the fight, but Claudius doesn't lose anything and he gains Hamlet's death either way. Maybe Hamlet will turn the tables and challenge Claudius to a duel instead of Laertes?

But Shakespeare is portraying events that represent awakening. Laertes is your worldly wisdom and professional expertise (symbolised by 'skill with the sword'). It is what we can loosely call true personality (though not entirely since Laertes is also headstrong and competitive). One of the

Laertes

significant stages of awakening is a confrontation between what is awakening, and the personal wisdom and good life principles you have always strived to live by, that is, true personality. These principles must now subject themselves to a firm and conscious aim – consistent and true. Such an aim can only belong to the Steward (your 'ruling faculty' that controls your psychology). And we shall see that Hamlet eventually proves himself to be up to the level of Steward. Certainly when he returns to Denmark he is much more self-assured.

CHAPTER 13
The Return of Hamlet

The audience may need some time to digest all the events that have happened rapidly one after the other and which are significant. Hamlet does return but first we see two gravediggers digging a hole. It is an interlude in the play, and the gravediggers are discussing Ophelia's death. They wonder whether it was suicide or an accident: if suicide, by church law she cannot be buried in a churchyard (which is where they are digging). The gravediggers are simple ordinary folk and their discussion is down to earth (indeed within it, since they are in a grave!).

No doubt, Shakespeare intended it that way. It is light relief, requiring no attention to any plot; they joke with words such as what I have just done, and ask each other riddles. This would appeal to many members of the audiences of his day who were ordinary folk themselves and could only afford to attend his performances standing on the ground in front of the stage. Indeed they were called 'groundlings' which was probably not lost on him as he used this fact in a visual pun (gravediggers dig in the ground, thus they are groundlings).

Finally, one of them leaves. The other continues

digging and singing to himself.

Hamlet and Horatio enter the scene.

On a more serious point, this is the first time in the play that Hamlet is portrayed away from the Castle of Elsinore (his exploits at sea are not shown, only described by letter to Horatio). Although this seems unremarkable, it actually shows that Hamlet is now *separate* from the castle, that is, the soul has separated itself from the rest of your everyday psychology and can thus observe it more abstractly.

Hamlet makes some comments to Horatio about a human skull that the gravedigger throws up, remarking that it could once have been a courtier or a politician or even a lord, but now is at the mercy of a gravedigger's dirty spade. Another skull is thrown up and he continues to muse about the difference between its owner in life and what it now is. Even if it had been Alexander the Great or Julius Caesar, it is now merely dirt that could be stopped in a hole to prevent draughts. It is clearly a sober observation about the emptiness of life, which is what started Hamlet on this whole quest in the first place.

He is equating life with death, even the life of a great statesman. But notice that Hamlet no longer decries and laments it. He has accepted the fact as a given.

Hamlet has changed; he has matured. His previous

bitter diatribes have been replaced by measured statements of fact. We can say that Steward is developing. The Steward in you does not partake in the antics of the many I's but remains detached from them. It is *outside of Elsinore*. In addition, take note that Hamlet's observations about life are being made in a cemetery, which is the place of death. In other words, Shakespeare is saying that all your other I's are in fact dead, and if you die to them, they will simply rot away to fossils. He emphasises this when the gravedigger throws up yet another skull and, when asked by Hamlet who it was, says it is Yorick the old King's jester. Hamlet pauses, pensively:

Alas poor Yorick! I knew him Horatio. (V,1,169)

He continues:

a fellow of infinite jest, of most excellent fancy.
he hath borne me on his back a thousand times.
And now how abhorred in my imagination it is!
My gorge rises at it.
(V,1,170)

He is describing the past attachment of your soul to your old self (Yorick), which *bore him on his back a thousand times* (carried you helplessly along), but which now repels him. It was clearly an attachment because he says:

Here hung those lips that I have kissed
I know not how oft.
(V,1,173)

Hamlet, Horatio and the Gravedigger

But now he can view the skull of Yorick in a detached way, as something separate from him. He mocks the skull – the old self – declaring its utter extinction:

> *Get you to my Lady's chamber and tell her,*
> *let her paint an inch thick,*
> *to this favour she must come.*
> (V,1,177)

Go tell a lady in her boudoir, that even if she applies cosmetics (airs and graces) an inch thick, yet she will end up like Yorick – a reference to 'woman' again, which is an allusion to the weakness in all of us to present ourselves to others as better than we really are.

Shakespeare uses the idea of cosmetics elsewhere to refer to the persona we show to others (false personality). No matter how good we are at acting this out – our charisma, or panache – it is worthless because it is *not yourself*:

> *…your painted counterfeit*
> *[…] Neither in inward worth nor outward fair,*
> *Can make you live yourself in eyes of men.*
> Sonnet XVI

In a way, Hamlet is recognising his old dead self for the first time, just like Horatio recognised the ghost of his dead father when he first saw him. The words: *I knew him, Horatio* are a direct reflection of what Horatio said to him: *I knew your father*. This underlines the close relationship between Hamlet and Horatio. We could say that Horatio is an understudy for the part of Hamlet, just like deputy steward is an understudy for Steward. I will say more about this later.

At this point they notice a funeral procession approaching the grave. It is Laertes, king, queen and court, with a priest and men carrying a coffin. Laertes disputes with the priest, who will not give Ophelia a fully complete rite of burial since her death is suspected of being suicide. Hamlet is shocked to find out the funeral is for Ophelia.

In a fit of passion Laertes jumps into the grave after Ophelia to embrace her one last time (the coffin being still open). His words are melodramatic and theatrical. Hamlet, inflamed by this show, also springs into the grave, declaring his feelings are contrary to the patent hypocrisy of Laertes:

> *I loved Ophelia. Forty thousand brothers*
> *could not with all their quantity of love*
> *make up my sum*
> (V,1,254)

The audience could be forgiven for being perplexed by this. First Hamlet had said to Ophelia in a letter (in II,2) *never doubt I love (thee)*; then he later said (in III,1): *I loved you not*. Now he is saying he loved her more than any brother!

It is yet another anomaly Shakespeare uses to alert us to look deeper – to follow the passage of awakening. In the beginning, the 'soul' (if it could be called so at that stage) is hardly independent, being merely a rejection of life and a desire for something more real. It is mixed up with the rest of your psychology; it is still attached to many parts – it 'loves' them (your innocent childhood part – Ophelia); while it is still proud of other parts (your philosophy of life, your mastery of certain skills, and your human wisdom – Laertes).

Then it starts to observe; sees more of what you really are; and finds things that horrify it. As already mentioned in the chapter *Hamlet Shows his Hand*, Hamlet says it like this:

> *I could accuse me of such things, that it were better my mother had not borne me.*
> (III,1,122)

And lacking comprehension at that stage, rejects everything, including Ophelia:

> *We are arrant knaves all: believe none of us.*
> *Go thy ways to a nunnery.*
> (III,1,128)

But now Hamlet is almost completely separate (except for one thing, as we shall see in a moment). He is almost a complete Steward and can perceive that his simple childhood essence was pure, though undeveloped. Now he loves Ophelia in a different way. In fact he has taken over her role, but now as a mature, comprehending essence. It is thus a different quality of love – knowing and understanding. That is why he indirectly accuses Laertes, who is her brother in the play, of merely heaping *quantities* of love on her, of little or no *quality*, and that he could easily match forty thousand of such brotherly quantities – an enormous figure used for emphasis (Until quite recently 'forty' has been commonly used in speech to mean very many). It also implies that Hamlet is prepared to *'bear it out – even to the edge of doom'* (Shakespeare's Sonnet 116 about love).

We can note here that *quantities* of love is something that corresponds to the nature of true personality (Laertes) since it knows well how to express itself in terms of quantities. In addition, true personality is well able to articulate the perceptions that actually arise from essence (Ophelia) and so in that sense it is its brother.

But here Hamlet is confronting Laertes. He taunts him, asking:

> *Dost thou come here to whine?*
> (V,1,262)

And again he asks (this is paraphrased for readability):

> *What would you do for your sister?*
> *Would you fast, weep, cry, eat a crocodile?*

For, he says:

> *I will do it.*

He is decrying Laertes' lack of substance. So we see here that *Steward* is still somewhat attached to this personality. It still thinks it is real. Your reasoning side, a side that has aided you for so long in your life, is also artificial and sooner or later has to be released. But it will not be easy. Shakespeare illustrates this by the coming duel between Hamlet and Laertes.

CHAPTER 14
Back in the Castle of Elsinore

Hamlet and Horatio have returned to the castle. Hamlet tells Horatio what happened on the ship to England. He shows him the letter Rosencrantz and Guildenstern had, commanding his swift beheading in England, not even waiting for *the grinding of the axe*, and tells him how he wrote a different one requesting their immediate execution instead, *no shriving-time allowed* (not allowing them time to confess or ask absolution).

Horatio is taken aback:

So Rosencrantz and Guildenstern go to't
(V,2,56)

he says - they go to their deaths. But Hamlet remarks:

They are not near my conscience (V,2,58)

We see again (like with the death of Polonius), the death of Hamlet's opponents does not affect him in the human sense.

He explains they brought their demise upon themselves by being servile to the king and standing between two such potent opposing forces (Hamlet and Claudius).

Here lies a clear indication that Hamlet has changed. He now finds himself equal in stature to his enemy, Claudius. He knows Claudius is a powerful adversary, having gone this far to get rid of him. But Hamlet has no compunction in thwarting him at every turn and will now stop at nothing to defeat him. Indeed he would be dammed himself if he did not stop him:

> *And is't not to be damned*
> *To let this canker of our nature come*
> *In further evil?*
> (V,2,68)

That is why Horatio exclaimed:

> *Why, what a King is this!* (V,2,63)

We can now equate Hamlet with *Steward* – the overarching determination within you to constantly reach for the Higher Self, while quashing the lower self at all opportunities. In the play this is done once only, when Claudius dies, but in fact you will have to do this countless times.

In this context, Rosencrantz and Guildenstern are merely I's used by the lower self to gain the Steward's death. That they were using the letter that Hamlet found shows that, although the lower self is stealthy, it does leave traces of its actions. It is the 'letters' that the Steward has to look for, because the lower self will always be one step ahead when the Steward is not on guard, that is, 'at sea'.

The play continues. Hamlet realises that in his encounter with Laertes he became too involved in his reactions to Laertes' show of grief:

> *But I am very sorry Horatio,*
> *That to Laertes I forgot myself*
> (V,2,76)

And he says he'll *court his favours* (he does not know yet that a duel has already been planned by the lower self, Claudius).

In a sense, the Steward and true personality are reflections of each other and have a certain affinity. The Steward serves your Higher Self by controlling your inner tendencies (such as imagination), and true personality serves your principles of life by controlling your behaviour. It is only if true personality tries to take the place of stewardship (symbolised in the play by Laertes dominating his sister Ophelia, and then displaying exaggerated bereavement at her funeral), that a conflict occurs.

Of course, at the beginning of awakening there is no steward (it has to be created in you), and so true personality has no inner counterpart. Your principles are the only worthy things at that stage. And they remain so but slowly a separate, more spiritual and comprehending part of you develops – the Steward.

It is beyond the scope of this book to go into the different stages of awakening in themselves. But we can also see here the role played by Horatio in the play. He studied at the same university of Wittenberg as Hamlet. Wittenberg is very appropriate because it was the place where the Reformation started in Europe in 1517, so we can link it to reformation of the soul. Shakespeare wrote the play later, the first performance of *Hamlet* being given in 1600.

So Horatio has been with Hamlet since the beginning and is, as already mentioned, an understudy for Hamlet's role, in other words he is a *deputy steward*. He understands the nature of Hamlet's quest but not its inner significance. But more than this, he is always available when Hamlet needs him. In the last scene, which we shall examine soon, Shakespeare combines his part with an even more significant role – that of the *nine-of-hearts**. The nine-of-hearts is the point in your essence where the original awakening spark glinted, and which brightens (after much time and effort) into a desire above all else for *conscious presence*. Yet it is not created, as Hamlet is, but already exists in essence, at first in embryonic form. Hamlet has to 'fan the flame'.

An insignificant courtier, Osric comes and, after being teased by Hamlet, delivers a message. The king has made a wager that Hamlet can beat Laertes in a duel of sword and dagger.

Then a lord arrives from the king asking if Hamlet could soon be ready for the match. Hamlet simply agrees to it. Horatio is alarmed by this sudden development – they are just not prepared for it, and he knows Laertes is a good swordsman.

After the lord leaves, he voices his doubt to Hamlet:

You will lose this wager, my lord (V,2,195)

But Hamlet will hear none of it. He has been practising, he says, and any misgivings are out of place.

Horatio insists that if Hamlet has any qualms at all, then he'll go and hold them off awhile saying Hamlet is not yet prepared.

Hamlet's reply is one of the more famous speeches in the play, now showing his full maturity as Steward:

Not a whit. We defy augury. There's a special providence in the fall of a sparrow.
If it be now,' tis not to come.
If it be not to come, it will be now.
If it be not now, yet it will come.
The readiness is all.
(V,2,205)

Hamlet is saying he does not live by reading omens (augury). Fate has already determined the hour of one's death and it cannot be changed. If it is now it won't be in the future, and vice versa – but if it is not now it is going to come anyway. So why worry about it? It is more important to be *ready* for this moment, whatever it brings.

Hamlet has thus completely transformed the initial condition of self-absorbed doubts and indecision expressed by:

To be or not to be, that is the question (III,1,56)

into a state of great certainty, even in a moment fraught with great personal peril:

The readiness is all (V,2,208)

This maturity can only come after great trials and suffering, and with a dogged perseverance.

CHAPTER 15
The Duel

The king, queen, Laertes and all the court arrive. Hamlet speaks to Laertes asking his forgiveness for all he has done to him (meaning the death of Polonius), and to his treatment of Laertes at the funeral. He cites his madness as the cause; he would not have done these things in his right mind; and he offers his love.

Laertes acknowledges Hamlet's plea comes from a genuine affection, and he accepts his offer of love, but he reserves his forgiveness according to the rules of honour, until some authority has advised him on how to proceed.

So we see here the basic difference between true personality and the steward. True personality acts according to rules of conduct that, with due thought, it has accepted as right and proper. The steward acts according to its own spiritual values of love and conscious presence.

They are given the fencing foils. Horatio will be Hamlet's Second, and Osric the courtier will be Laertes' Second.

Claudius now declares that if Hamlet wins the first hit he will drink to him and then toss a priceless jewel – his ring – into the goblet as a reward before giving it to him (in fact the ring contains a compartment filled with the poison).

The duel begins. The two men are evenly matched so it goes on for a while. Hamlet makes a hit on Laertes. Claudius drinks to him, throws the jewel (with the poison) into the chalice and offers it to him. Hamlet declines, saying he will wait until the bout is over.

Laertes plays around with Hamlet and only hits him slightly, feeling a twinge of conscience. But a hit is declared and there is some discussion. Gertrude wants to encourage Hamlet, so she drinks to him from the cup, not knowing it is poisoned. Claudius, alarmed, tries to stop her, but he is too late.

Hamlet teases Laertes for the lightness of the hit saying, *You but dally*, and that Laertes should lunge with his best force.

They engage again and Laertes strikes him with the deadly point of the sword. Hamlet is wounded, but does not fall immediately. They scuffle and the swords are inadvertently exchanged, so that now, Hamlet unknowingly holds the poisoned sword. He pierces Laertes with it.

Laertes falls.

At that moment Gertrude cries out suddenly. Affected by the poison she falls to the floor, dying.

In quick order, three people have fallen. Horatio

tends to Hamlet, Osric first calls out for help for Gertrude, and then tends to Laertes.

Laertes, true to his nature, declares he has been justly killed by his own treachery.

Claudius, covering his tracks, says Gertrude has only fainted because of the sight of blood. But Gertrude cries out:

> *No, no, the drink, the drink –*
> *Oh my dear Hamlet –*
> *The drink, the drink! I am poisoned.*
> (V,2,295)

At last Hamlet sees treachery and orders all the doors closed.

At this point Laertes confesses to Hamlet that the sword was tipped, that Hamlet has only a half hour to live, and that both he and Laertes, plus Gertrude are poisoned. He begs his forgiveness, saying that the king was behind all the treachery.

Hamlet, already flushed with the fighting, is incensed and strides over to Claudius thrusting his sword into him. Then he forces the poison down his throat, killing him. Laertes seeing it exclaims *He is justly served by his own poison*. Laertes then dies.

So Claudius has finally died. But also have Gertrude and Laertes. And pretty soon Hamlet will die too.

This scene of wholesale murder is at once breathtaking and perplexing. One might not have expected so many deaths in quick succession of nearly all the main characters, not to mention that the 'hero' himself is also about to die.

Several things need to be said about this. First of all, the duel shows that the final struggle of the Steward (Hamlet) is with true personality, one's own reason (Laertes), which is turned outward to life. It is the effort to abandon all you believed in (which in a sense, defines who you are) in submission to your overriding focus on pure conscious presence.

Secondly, Hamlet, even though he was poisoned first, is the last one to die. The Steward is not so much affected by the 'poison' of the lower self as are the other parts. It is more separate from the rest of you and does not believe the I's.

Thirdly, the lower self has *no conscience*. Claudius is not concerned with Gertrude's life. He is more concerned with his own survival, hence his words that she was only fainting. Also, in the 'praying' scene of Act III scene 3 Claudius only goes through the act of conscience. Likewise in us, the lower self can make us believe we have a conscience about something, but it is only guilt, be it ever so mild – which is the fear of being found out and punished.

Fourthly, it is clear that the lower self uses other parts to do its dirty work but if they fail, it has a plan-B. Claudius engaged Laertes to kill Hamlet, but has the poison cup to make sure.

But here the poison itself represents something significant in our psychology, for whenever we experience strong negative emotions we feel poisoned. And the poison affects all our good thoughts (Laertes) and feelings of right and wrong (Gertrude).

Finally, the force of your aim and efforts to gain conscious presence is counteracted by an almost equal and opposite force of the lower self. The stronger you are (the stronger your Steward), the stronger the opposing forces mustered by the lower self. That is why in this play Gertrude (your emotional sense of right living, or feminine dominance), and Laertes (your principles and knowledge of truth) both have to go if Claudius is to be killed.

Hamlet forces the poison on Claudius

CHAPTER 16
The Death of Hamlet

Only Hamlet and Horatio are left alive. Hamlet feels the onset of death. He says he could tell Horatio many things but now the time is too short – a distinct reference to what many people feel on the point of death. In an attempt to hasten it he tries to take the cup from Horatio, but Horatio resists saying that he is prepared to take the poison instead (an honourable gesture but poignantly useless). Hamlet grabs the cup and drinks.

Hamlet then tells Horatio something significant. We know it is significant because he tells him three separate times. First he says:

> *Thou livest. Report me and my cause aright*
> *To the unsatisfied* (V,2,325)

Tell those who doubt my motives what really happened. The second time is after the exchange over the cup of poison:

> *And in this harsh world of pain,*
> *Tell my story.* (V,2,334)

The third time is not quite yet, because now Prince Fortinbras (who you remember was passing through Denmark to attack Poland), suddenly arrives on the scene.

Hamlet recognises him. He is the one for whom Hamlet has avenged his father and has given up his life, though he does not say it quite like that. Rather he says that Fortinbras is the one on whom the *light of kingship* now shines:

> *I do prophesy the election lights on Fortinbras*
> *He has my dying voice* (V,2,341)

So, Fortinbras takes over 'the voice' from Hamlet.

And then Hamlet asks Horatio for the third time to tell all that happened (paraphrased for readability):

> *So tell him all the events that happened,*
> *with all their causes.* (V,2,343)

He has thus charged Horatio to make great efforts to tell the whole story of Hamlet after he has died.

Dying in the arms of his bosom friend, Hamlet's very last words are:

> *The rest is Silence.* (V,2,344)

Here are four words. It is very clear and simple, and it is more significant than it appears.

'Rest' on a literal level is rest after death. On a deeper level it is what follows 'death'. But is it what follows for Hamlet or is it what follows for everyone else? For Hamlet it is clear. For the audience it might mean "there is no more to be said", but Shakespeare does say more things, so that's not it.

For us what follows the "death of the steward" is *silence*. But it is not death – because *none of the deaths* of the characters in this play mean actual death. Their 'deaths' mean they have been overcome. And the death of the steward means that even the steward has to give up his existence to allow the Higher Self to appear. He has to do that intentionally, so to say consciously. It is a bowing-down and a diminishing of the sense of existence all the way down to a complete nothingness.

This is because the quality of the Higher Self is *conscious silence* and *emptiness*. It is in a state of rest. There is no mental activity; there are no words, no thoughts, and no feelings. Yet there is great alertness and awareness. All can be clearly seen, heard, felt, smelled and tasted, including yourself. All is clear and understood.

This state can be held, typically for a period of four breaths, but then usually the first stirrings of lower parts appear again. That is why the use of four words is significant in the text. *The rest is Silence* actually depicts this state and its length.

In the play as I have mentioned often, all this happens once, but for you it happens many times, and each time you must bring your Hamlet (as quickly as you can) from a state of vagueness and indecision (as in *To be or not to be* – six short words) all the way to the full state of *readiness*. You can do this (after much practice) by saying six short words, such as those just given (or another six words which are significant for you, such as the first words of the Lord's prayer), while at the same time trying as much as you can to be present to them and to yourself. On the last word you finally let everything go and 'die' completely in the face of your God, your Higher Self.

In the play then, after Hamlet dies, Horatio says *Good Night Sweet Prince*, which is also four words, and he says he has a story for everyone. Many momentous things have happened and he can tell them everything.

Fortinbras is accompanied by English ambassadors and they fret that they cannot deliver their message from England (that Rosencrantz and Guildenstern have been put to death). This means that all the I's against awakening have disappeared, and there are no other I's that wish to hear about them.

Fortinbras declares he has come to reclaim what was rightfully his and wishes to hear the story from Horatio. Meanwhile he assigns four unnamed captains (meaning again the four silent breaths) to carry the body of Hamlet away *like a soldier*, for he has proved himself *most royal* (a most perfect steward). Fortinbras then takes over the court.

Fortinbras symbolises the Higher Self – but he is both a regeneration of Hamlet's father, Hamlet, and a restoration of his own father, Fortinbras.

So all has been restored to what it was. The true spiritual nature of man, in us when we are born, genetic, metaphysical, and celestial, has to be brought to fruition, through a struggle with our own wilful, lower tendencies. The struggle is arduous and long, and involves many 'deaths'. But as Paul says in 1 Corinthians 15:55:

> *Death is swallowed up in victory,*
> *Oh death, where is thy sting?*
> *Oh grave, where is thy victory?*

CHAPTER 17
The End?

So at the end our hero Hamlet dies and Fortinbras takes back what is his right – the one left standing takes all.

This is very similar to what happened in the original battle between the great King Hamlet (our Hamlet's father), and the great King Fortinbras (our Fortinbras' father), before the play started (which was actually narrated by Horatio at the beginning of the play).

The great King Hamlet had agreed at that time to "*a sealed compact*" with the great King Fortinbras that whoever vanquished the other would take all, and whoever lost the battle would

> *forfeit with his life all those his lands*
> *which he stood seized of, to the conqueror* (I,1,88)

So now it looks like the tables are turned – Fortinbras (who we have equated to the Higher Self) has replaced all lower parts and takes all. The last words of the Lord's Prayer are uttered when one has given all of oneself up to the higher God: *For thine is the Kingdom, the Power and the Glory.* Fortinbras has the Kingdom (of Hamlet) and the Power. And he has the Glory – a word signifying *divine and conscious presence.* Amen.

But is that the end? No, because divine conscious presence has no end. The play goes on. If you remember, just before he died, *Hamlet* urged Horatio:

> *In this harsh world draw thy breath in pain,*
> *To tell my story.* (V,2,334)

Horatio is thus the key, the connector, the figure who will start again, just like the nine-of-hearts.

Horatio will tell the same story again someday to some watchmen – only this time it will be how Fortinbras vanquished Hamlet. Fortinbras will have a son who will see his father removed by a villain. The son of Fortinbras will slowly begin to realise what has happened; he will struggle with himself; and finally he will overcome all his obstacles and then die. And then a new Hamlet will appear and reclaim his right.

And all through this Horatio will be there, listening, watching, supporting and telling the eternal story to the next Hamlet and the next Fortinbras – world without end. Amen.

Hamlet was not just a play. It was a flashback to the previous time you awakened.

Summary of Characters and Places

Characters

Hamlet Begins as a felt need to awaken, that is, *magnetic centre*. As the play progresses he gathers strength and substance, until finally he reaches the level of *Steward*. But he is under the power of the *Lower Self* for most of play.

The Ghost Represents the original true state of each of us, but it has been buried ('killed') by the time of adulthood. His 'death' reflects the Fall of Man (the poison in the ear symbolises Adam listening to the words of the serpent in the garden of Eden).

Horatio Hamlet's staunch and closest friend. Honest, loyal and supportive. He represents largely the *deputy steward*, as an understudy of steward, putting things in order, and knowing the background of Hamlet's plight. He also has, and later develops, what can be likened to the *nine-of-hearts* (supporting truth, and recognising the Higher).

(Although the *nine-of-hearts* is commonly portrayed as a woman, here it is a man to avoid romantic overtones. Even a sister would need support from the hero and not vice-versa).

Horatio is *Nine-of-hearts* because he: 1) recognises the Ghost clearly (the Higher); 2) does not die like the other characters; 3) supports the dying Hamlet; 4) can then tell the whole story to the world,; and 5) accepts the arrival of Fortinbras (Higher Self)

Claudius Has taken over the Kingship by murdering his brother. Later, he fears Hamlet will reveal his crime and so plots to have him killed (to quash the awakening soul). Claudius clearly represents the *lower self*, which has an insatiable drive for Self-Gratification and control over your psyche.

Gertrude The Queen, mother of Hamlet and swiftly married to Claudius after her husband's death. Represents an uneducated emotional centre (especially the Queen-of-Hearts), and that which underlies *feminine dominance* (the need for moral support, security, love and comfort), and therefore is under the power of the lower self (Claudius).

Ophelia Daughter of Polonius. Represents suppressed and undeveloped *Essence* - Innocence, naivety, immaturity, vulnerability, believing anything she is told. She is all your simple perceptions remaining since childhood – totally dominated by her father Polonius, and brother Laertes. Later, Hamlet as a mature steward, takes over her role.

Polonius The King's Chief Counsellor. He is the Imaginary Picture of oneself, superficial thinking, vanity and pride – thus *False Personality*.

Laertes Ophelia's brother and son of Polonius. He is the reasoning personality– I's protecting essence (Ophelia). Has good values and is worldly-wise. He is close to, but not exactly *True Personality* since he is turned entirely towards life and ambitions (represented by 'France').

Rosencranz and Guildenstern Two men of court with dubious morals, not very bright, and entirely superficial. Exploited by the lower self to get rid of Hamlet. They represent the Rosicrucians & Freemasons (see Appendix A) – thus they are *B-Influence* or *Relative Awakening*.

Fortinbras Appears when all the characters except Horatio have died and takes over the court of Elsinore. He is Noble, honourable, courageous. He represents the *Higher Self*, or Conscious Presence.

Places

Denmark Symbolises your whole inner world and your inner impression of the external world. Thus it is the world of your psyche in the play, the landscape of Hamlet's inner strife

Elsinore The castle of Elsinore. This represents your being, the sum total of your psychology.

England Symbolises the world of life – the world of the Instinctive Centre and its needs and urges. (*A-Influence*)

France This is professional life; earning a living; having ambition; seeking your fortune; being successful.

Appendix A
Rosencrantz and Guildenstern

It is quite possible that Shakespeare was making a secondary point in his play by including these ineffective characters and that he was making fun of secret societies of his day. He was showing these societies as pursuing esoteric ideas and symbolism, but as entirely missing the point of spirituality.

Shakespeare was a master of words and these two names show his skill. Both names were of well-known rich Danish Families of the time and so they fit the play perfectly. But the name Rosencrantz might be derived from Christian Rosenkreuz who purportedly founded the Order of Rosicrucians in the 15th century. Shakespeare needed only to replace two letters to change Rosenkreuz - "Rosy Cross" to Rosencrantz - "Rosy Wreath", which signifies death. He could thus be saying that Rosicrucianism does not lead to eternal life, but to death.

Guildenstern was also a well-known Danish family name, but here Shakespeare may have derived it from a name with one letter less, Guildensten.

This is made up of "Guilden", trades-groups, and "sten", the Danish word for "stone". Thus we have the Guilds of Stone-men - Stonemasons. Could this not refer to the Freemasons, who in the late 1500s were already developing their philosophy and rituals?

If this conjecture is valid then these two characters, Rosencrantz and Guildenstern, represent the Rosicrucians and Freemasons and the superficiality of rituals and discussion.

Glossary

A-Influence – One of A- B- and C-Influences, A-influence denotes the Influences that operate in ordinary daily life. These are concerned with home, jobs, marriage, relationships, career, success, family, health, status, dignity, and reputation. This is represented by *England* in the play.

Being –The degree to which you can be conscious of yourself and your surroundings, and also to act intentionally according to your understanding, regardless of ingrained personal habits and tendencies, sometimes in conditions of great pressure. This is represented by the *Castle of Elsinore* in the play.

B-Influence – One of A- B- and C-Influences, B-influence denotes the Influences that originally came from conscious sources but which have since become mixed up with imagination or *A-Influence*. Also, influences which purport to be conscious but which are just inventions. Represented by Rosencrantz and Guildenstern in the play. See Appendix A.

C-Influence – One of A- B- and C-Influences, C-influence denotes Direct Conscious influences, coming either from a conscious teacher or from conscious beings at celestial levels. C-Influence always impels one to a greater awareness of one's self in one's surroundings, whether pleasant or not. This is represented by the Ghost in the play, though this is only a partial representation of these. See also *Conscience* below.

Conscience – A faculty normally buried, which appears only in tense moments of personal moral indecision, prompting as to what is right action for you personally (usually, but not always, something you do not wish to do). It is represented by the Ghost in the play. See also *C-Influence* above.

Conscious Presence –A condition in which your *Higher Self*, is in control of all lower functions including the lower self, is totally aware of its surroundings and their true nature, and is fully aware of itself. The state can be produced after long work, by the calming of all lower functions, gathering all of one's being, and by submitting to the will of what is higher.

Deputy Steward – A certain ability to control and organise inner parts of yourself following the understanding of what you wish in conscious evolution. It can tell which *I's* (thoughts and feelings) are more real, and which are not worth believing.

Essence –The most real part of your ordinary psychology. It is the part you were born with, consisting of talents and tendencies specific to you. It is how you saw things as a child. Although the talents develop by being used, essence itself becomes largely covered over as you grow up, firstly by attitudes imposed on it by its parents and teachers, and later by social norms. If you are intent on awakening, it can, after being educated, become the active force in your efforts to become conscious. In this sense, Hamlet is the educated essence.

False Personality - This is your public face, your opinions, postures, mannerisms and attitudes that have been automatically and unconsciously formed mostly by imitation or opposition. It is mostly concerned with maintaining your imaginary picture of yourself. See *Imaginary Picture*.

Feminine Dominance – The need and desire to be accepted in society, even on a minute by minute basis, in terms of social customs and morality, especially with regard to family values. This varies from country to country. It is "feminine" because 1) you first learned your idea of "right and wrong" behaviour from your mother, and indeed most of your relationship to your mother is part of this; and 2) you feel this dominance in a passive way – that is to say, from within yourself – there being usually no external commands.

Fundamental Personal Aim – An aim which starts as a desire to discover the meaning of your life. Then it becomes *magnetic centre*, which we see in Hamlet in the first part of the play (up to "To

Be of not to Be"), which gathers all knowledge about awakening (Hamlet at the university of WittenBerg). Finally it develops into a Permanent Aim to become conscious.

Higher Centres – Two centres which are only accessible in the state of *Conscious Presence*, as opposed to the *Lower Centres* which are our ordinary brains for life.

Higher Self – The Spirit in each human being. It is at first no more than a principle, easily buried and forgotten. Or it may have been simply never recognised, and ultimately totally destroyed. But Esoteric school teaches that to reach it, you first have to create a soul from, as it were, nothing. When it is fully developed, this soul which we can then call *Steward*, works by overcoming the other parts of your psychology, one by one (indicated in the play by the death of each character), finally achieving superiority over your *Lower Self* (this is Claudius in the play). The steward then has to recede and allow the Higher Self to take its rightful place. In the play this is portrayed by the death of Hamlet and the arrival of Fortinbras.

Imaginary Picture – The image a person has about themselves that they believe or wish to believe, and which they wish other people to see and believe also.

'I's – Individual Thoughts, Feelings, Impulses or Urges which occur in a constant stream in our psychology. They are called 'I's because we assume for each one of them, that it is 'I' who is thinking, doing or feeling. Nothing is further from the truth because these are just individual responses to stimuli which either impact us from outside or come from previous I's.

Inner Considering – Concern or worry about what the other person expects of you or thinks of you. It is usually subconsciously felt and is connected with your imaginary picture of yourself. See *Imaginary Picture*.

Lower centres – Four brains which exist in everyone. These are: instinctive centre (bodily functions, survival, fitness, strength, power and cunning); moving centre (movements, perception of space, athleticism, but also engineering and technology); intellectual centre (ideas, discussion, language, philosophy) ; and emotional centre (feelings, relationships, drama, poetry and art).

Lower Self – The intelligence in the intellectual part of the instinctive centre that is determined to prevent consistent efforts to be *consciously present*, although it will allow short periods of success. This intelligence normally rules the everyday person you are, and does not wish to give up its power. It will employ all the lower centres (see *Lower Centres*) to achieve its purpose, particularly the emotional centre.

Magnetic Centre – The seed of the soul which starts off by seeking knowledge about celestial matters and things beyond everyday life. It gravitates to, and attracts, other people who are also seeking these things. In the play, Hamlet gains this knowledge in the University of Wittenberg, where the European reformation started (so – reformation of the soul).

Nine-of-hearts – Technically, this is one of the 52 playing cards, each one denoting a separate element of our psychology that we are all born with. It is the element in the intellectual part of the Emotional centre which reveres the *Higher Self* and values all efforts to reach it. It is what always wishes to awaken, and it provides the drive which allows the *Steward* to act in accordance with that wish.

Non-existence – A very passive character trait in some people whereby they habitually let other people take decisions for them in all matters – even, in some cases, the choice of what to eat. At first, such a person seems very agreeable because they agree with everything you say.

Objective Art – That kind of art which was created to impact the *Higher Self*. This art, although it can also contain many other features and usually does, includes an element that evokes a sense of mystery or other-worldliness. Examples are: The great Pyramid of Egypt; the Taj Mahal; the Mona Lisa; The Lord's Prayer; and Shakespeare's *Hamlet* itself.

Presence, being present – The sense of being alive to what is before you, while also being aware of your inner reactions, associations and tendencies. See *Conscious Presence*.

Relative Awakening – A condition in which you have esoteric knowledge – of yourself and things not in the normal stream of life – but you are still not consciously present.

Self Remembering (or Remembering Yourself) – The action of bringing attention to your surroundings and dividing it so that some attention is simultaneously directed to yourself. See also *Being Present* and *Conscious Presence*.

Separating, Separation – The withdrawal of the feeling of 'self' from your *lower self* and observing it as though it were somebody else.

Shock – Something that stimulates a moment of *Conscious Presence* in you. It is not usually a dramatic moment of discomfort, although in rare cases it could be.

Steward – An advanced development arising from *essence*, once one's work has reached a high enough level. Steward understands fully the need for engaging the *Higher Self* in all circumstances. As it grows stronger it acquires control over one's *Lower Self*, and is active in holding *Conscious Presence* for progressively longer periods of time.

True Personality – All the personal observations, verifications, understandings and wisdom regarding one's life and other people's lives. It is that side of us which tries to consider everything with as much reason and common sense as we can muster.

Bibliography

The books by Rodney Collin may be out of print. *In Search of the Miraculous* by P.D. Ouspensky, *Self-Remembering* by Robert Earl Burton, and *Creating a Soul* by Girard Haven, give excellent coverage of the ideas behind the Fourth Way, and *The Art of Presence* by Girard Haven gives an up to date exposition of the methods used by esoteric schools since ancient times.

Robert Earl Burton   *Self-Remembering* (Globe Press Books, New York, 1991)

Rodney Collin   *The Theory of Celestial Influence* (Vincent Stuart, London 1954)

-------------------   *The Theory of Conscious Harmony* (Watkins, London 1958)

-------------------   *The Theory of Eternal Life* (By the Way Books, Sacramento, CA)

Georg I. Gurdjieff   *Beelzebub's Tales to His Grandson* (Arkana, New York, 1992)

-------------------   *Meetings with Remarkable Men* (Arkana, New York, 1985)

-------------------   *Life is Real Only Then, When "I Am"* (Arkana, New York, 1999)

―――――――――――― *Views from the Real World* (Penguin Compass, New York, 1984)

Girard Haven   *The Art of Presence* (Blue Logic Publications, Oregon House, CA, 2010)

―――――――――――― *The Prize is Eternity* (Ulysses Books, Oregon House, CA, 2002)

―――――――――――― *Creating a Soul* (Ulysses Books, Oregon House, CA, 1999)

Martin Lings The Secret of Shakespeare (Inner Traditions International Ltd., New York, 1984)

P. D. Ouspensky   *Conscience* (Routledge & Kegan Paul, London, 1979)

―――――――――――― *The Fourth Way* (Vintage Books, New York, 1971)

―――――――――――― *In Search of the Miraculous* (Routledge & Kegan Paul, London, 1957)

―――――――――――― *The Psychology of Man's Possible Evolution*   (Vintage Books, New York, 1981)

Image Attributions

Illustration by Kevin Watts:
>Cover
>Elsinore Castle
>Claudius tries to pray
>Ophelia
>Laertes
>Hamlet and the Gravedigger
>Hamlet forces the poison on Claudius

In general, unless otherwise indicated, all other images are used under Royalty Free ("RF") and Wikimedia Commons Public Domain Licenses ("PD").

>*Mountain seen through temple window -Machu Picchu*
>Photo taken by the author
>
>*Queen Gertrude*   painted by Edwin Abbey 1885
>Courtesy Wikimedia Commons Public Domain. US: {PD-1996}
>
>*Hamlet*   Henry Irving 1888 – Courtesy Wikimedia Commons
>Public Domain. US: {PD-1996}
>
>*Ophelia faces Hamlet*   Courtesy Wikimedia Commons
>Public Domain. US: {PD-1996}
>
>*Hamlet and the ghost of his father* -- from a production of Hamlet, University of Miami Ring Theatre 2009. Photograph courtesy of: Kent Lantaff, General Manager (and photographer)

The Fellowship of Friends

The Fellowship of Friends is a group dedicated to Conscious Presence, founded in 1970 by Robert Earl Burton, which uses practical and proven methods for generating self-awareness and conscious presence. While much of its knowledge is based on the System of G.I. Gurdjieff and P.D. Ouspensky, its methods now come from traditional esoteric schools of great antiquity, which all teach the same thing, and are very direct.

It has many national centres throughout the Americas, Europe, Asia, North Africa, and the Far East, though its heart lies in a community in the foothills of the Sierra Nevada Mountains in California. Students are continually circulating among all these centres.

More information can be found by visiting the web-site:

http://www.livingpresence.com/

where a full explanation of its practises can be found together with many suggestions for further reading. There is a monthly newsletter to which you can subscribe, which is free and holds no obligation. The site also tells you how to make contact with one of its centres, should you be interested in the possibility of joining the School.

http://bluelogic.us/

www.ingramcontent.com/pod-product-compliance
Ingram Content Group UK Ltd.
Pitfield, Milton Keynes, MK11 3LW, UK
UKHW022121230426
12048UKWH00011BA/643

9 780976 973287